ARTHUR STREETON 1867 - 1943

A Biographical Sketch
By Geoffrey Dutton

Famous Australian Art Series

Oz Publishing Co.

Front Cover:

Detail from:
*Near Streeton's Camp
at Sirius Cove, 1892*
oil on canvas
30.4 x 22.7 cm
Bequest of Howard Hinton 1948
Collection: New England Regional Art Museum,
Armidale, N.S.W.
Reproduced by permission of Oliver Streeton
Full colour plate of Near Streeton's Camp
at Sirius Cove, 1892 on page 31.

ARTHUR STREETON
1867-1943

Smike Streeton, age 24, 1891

Portrait of Arthur Streeton
by Tom Roberts
oil on canvas
45.7 x 35.7 cm
Purchased 1945
Collection: Art Gallery of New South Wales

GEOFFREY DUTTON

First published in 1987
By Oz Publishing Co., Pty Ltd.
P.O. Box 1083, Milton Centre, Brisbane.
Reprinted 1988

Text © Geoffrey Dutton

National Library of Australia
Cataloguing-in-Publication data
ISBN 0 947207 04 X
1. Famous Australian Art
2. Arthur Streeton
3. Geoffrey Dutton
4. Famous Australian Art Series

OZ PUBLISHING CO., PTY LTD
P.O. Box 1083,
Milton Centre.
Brisbane, Qld. 4064

Phototypesetting by
S&M, Brisbane.

Colour Separations by
Haighs Foto Art, Brisbane.

Printed by
Polygraphics Pty. Ltd. Brisbane.

Bound by
Podlich Enterprises, Brisbane.

1788-1988

"This publication has been endorsed by The Australian Bicentennial
Authority to celebrate Australia's Bicentenary in 1988".

CONTENTS

TEXT

ILLUSTRATIONS

INTRODUCTION

As a young man, Arthur Streeton was in love with the Australian landscape with a poetic intensity that challenged him to interpret it as no one else had been able to do. Even more than his friends, Roberts, McCubbin and Conder, he saw something entirely new to be painted, something as fresh as every day's sunlight. All through his working life as an artist Streeton used a palette on which he had painted a shining sun; he even had his linen marked with the same device.

He first saw the Australian day on 8th of April 1867, at Mt Duneed near Geelong in Victoria. His father was an English schoolteacher who had emigrated in 1854; he lived to be 102. Arthur was the fourth child of a family of seven. Maybe his father helped him develop his passion for poetry; he is always quoting it in his letters, and some of the titles of his most famous works are taken from poems. He did not attempt to become a poet, but he was a remarkable writer of prose. His letters are vivid and individual, particularly those addressed to Tom Roberts.

A BIOGRAPHICAL SKETCH

In 1875 the Streetons moved to South Yarra in Melbourne, and Arthur went to the Punt Road State School. He left school at the age of 13 and went to work as a clerk for a firm importing spirits; he then worked in a soft-goods firm. From 1884 to 1888 he attended night classes at the Melbourne National Gallery School, where he studied design under McCubbin. He showed enough artistic talent for him to be taken on as an apprentice with Troedel & Cooper, lithographers, in 1886.

In the 1886–7 summer the artist Frederick McCubbin came across the 19-year old Streeton painting a seascape at Beaumaris, and was so impressed that he asked Streeton to join the Box Hill camp with his friends Tom Roberts and Louis Abrahams. Streeton was nicknamed 'Smike' after the character in Dickens' *Nicholas Nickleby*, probably because of his slight build. Roberts was 'Bulldog' and McCubbin 'the Prof'. A portrait of Streeton by Roberts, and a contemporary photograph, show a young man with an eager, thoughtful face, the chin accentuated by a pointed beard.

Although Streeton was not associated with the Box Hill camp until the second year of its existence, it made a deep impression on him. When he was in London in 1901 he wrote to McCubbin: 'I close my eyes and see again the ... black wattles and ti tree down by the creek, the Houstons (sic) cabin, the messmate tree and its misteltoe and horehound patch beneath, the run for trains on Sunday night and Prof far up ahead, mopping his brow near Jack Ganges' — the flush over the Dandenongs and the quiet and grey valley beyond White Horse Road toward Macedon'.

Charles Conder was also painting at the Box Hill camp, and Streeton was deeply impressed by the young English artist's ideas. Streeton also painted near Heidelberg with a fellow-student, David Davies, whose brother-in-law (also called Davies) lent Streeton a rambling, almost derelict weatherboard house at Eaglemont.

Streeton spent the first night there alone 'excepting for the caretaker at the farther end of the house, ... my boots and coat for a pillow. I slept upon the floor, the rooms being bare of furniture. The whole place was creaking and ghostly . . . But tobacco and wine weighed healthily against the darkness and solitude.'

Streeton invited other artists to join him at Eaglemont, and soon a group of friends, including Roberts and Conder, established themselves to paint, and teach art to the young ladies who came out at weekends. A visiting American art critic, Sidney Dickinson, called them the 'Heidelberg School'.

Conder later wrote to Roberts: 'I feel more than sorry that (those) days are over, because nothing can exceed the pleasures of that last summer, when I fancy all of us lost the 'Ego' somewhat of our natures in looking at what was Nature's best art and ideality. Give me one summer again with yourself and Streeton — the same long evenings, songs, dirty plates, and last pink skies'.

At Eaglemont in 1889 Streeton painted a long, light-filled landscape called *Golden Summer*; Conder took it with him to London in 1890, and it was exhibited at the Old Salon in Paris in 1892 and bought by an English collector.

Streeton painted a high-keyed oil sketch for *Golden Summer* in the full sunlight. He wrote to Tom Roberts: 'Oh, the long, hot day. Oh, the gift of appreciation. I sit on our hill of gold, on the north side; the wind seems sunburnt and fiery as it runs though my beard. Yes, rather, see, look here: north-east the very long divide is beautiful, warm blue, far, far away, all dreaming and remote. Now to the east a little . . . Yes, I sit here in the upper circle surrounded by copper and gold, and smile joy (sic) under my fly net as all the light, glory and quivering brightness passes slowly and freely before my eyes'.

Streeton had certainly been studying reproductions of Corot and Millet, and trying to learn what he could about French Impressionism, but he was finding his feet as a painter of Australian light and colour. In fact, he was up and running.

The Heidleberg artists had combined to make up the 9 x 5 Impression Exhibition that scandalized Melbourne in 1889. (The paintings in the exhibition were mostly on cedar cigar box lids, 9 x 5 inches, supplied by Abrahams of the original Box Hill group, whose

Facing Page:

Early Summer~Gorse in Bloom, 1888

oil on canvas
56.2 x 100.6 cm
Art Gallery of South Australia Foundation 1892
Collection: Art Gallery of South Australia
Reproduced by permission of Oliver Streeton

father had a tobacco business). Streeton exhibited forty paintings. The prices in the show were mostly from one to three guineas, and the most expensive picture was nine guineas.

The catalogue, prettily designed by Conder, began with a quotation from Gerome: 'When you draw, form is the most important thing; but in painting the first thing to look for is the general impression of colour'. It then addressed the public: 'An Effect is only momentary; so an impressionist tries to find his place. Two half-hours are never alike, and he who tries to paint a sunset on two successive evenings, must be more or less painting from memory. So, in these works, it has been the object of the artists to render faithfully, and thus obtain first records of effects widely differing, and often of very fleeting character'.

Melbourne's leading art critic, James Smith of the *Argus*, who was also a very influential Gallery Trustee, did not care for the Impressions. 'The modern impressionist asks you to see pictures in splashes of colour, in slap-dash brushwork, and in sleight-of-hand

Facing Page:

The Clearing, Gembrook, 1888

oil on canvas
25.4 x 45.7 cm
Felton Bequest 1942
Collection: National Gallery of Victoria
Reproduced by permission of Oliver Streeton

methods of execution leading to the proposition of pictorial conundrums, which would baffle solution if there were no label or catalogue'.

The 9 x 5 Exhibition sold very well, but of course at those prices there was very little money in it for the artists. (Today a really fine 9 x 5 Roberts or Streeton might fetch $200,000).

Ever since the opening of The Centennial Exhibition in 1888, which covered an area of thirty three acres, including the largest display of local and imported art ever seen in Australia, Melbourne had been congratulating itself as a patron of the arts. On 5 May 1888 an *Argus* journalist wrote: 'Dense crowds of people might be seen gathering on every hand, all armed with catalogues and eagerly discussing the prospects of Australian art . . . Indeed the popularity of art may be described as second only to that of football and negro minstrelsy, and well above cricket, or even land sales'.

In fact, those with plenty of money, the squatters and business men, did not buy Australian art, but wasted their riches on rubbish

Facing Page:

Silver Wattle, 1888

watercolour on paper
30 x 50 cm
Private Collection
Reproduced by permission of Oliver Streeton

Silver Wattle.

Arthur Streeton

Mch 88

sent out by London dealers. The work of the Heidelberg painters, when it sold at all, was bought by a small group of university and professional people; a notable patron was Pinschof, the Austro-Hungarian Consul. The National Gallery gave them very little support, and the same was true for the other State Galleries.

As Streeton wrote, a few years later, to Roberts: 'This country is full of wealth, but somehow can't afford artists yet. Why, dammit, bricklayers, scene shifters, office boys, all get their work recognized and are able to go on — and if I were recognized more I could PAINT MORE'.

It was Sydney, not Melbourne that gave Streeton his first chance. In 1890 he exhibited *Still glides the stream, and shall for ever glide* (originally called 'An Australian Gloaming', at the Winter Exhibition of the Victorian Artists' Society). The quotation 'Still glides the Stream', comes from a poem by Wordsworth. It is a lovely, serene and warm painting of the Yarra river lazing across the flats near Heidelberg, with a hint of Corot in the otherwise Australian trees. The

Facing Page:

The Yarra, Ivanhoe, 1888

oil on canvas
31.7 x 62.5 cm
Collection: Bendigo Art Gallery
Reproduced by permission of Oliver Streeton

Art Gallery of New South Wales bought the painting for £70.

With some money in his pocket at last, Streeton headed for Sydney. Roberts followed him and they settled by the Harbour at Curlew Camp, Little Sirius Cove. They were very poor, but happy to be working together once again. The financial support from Sydney was only temporary. Streeton exhibited some Harbour paintings at the Art Society of New South Wales, but failed to sell any.

For the next two years he worked in Sydney and in the Blue Mountains. Some of his most vivid letters, to McCubbin and Roberts, describe the blasting of Lapstone railway tunnel through the mountainside in 1981. Streeton saw the work of the men as heroic, in a marvellous frame of rock, and one of his finest paintings, *Fire's On*, came from his observations of the blasting. One day when he was sketching, a man was killed under a fall of rock. 'He lies hidden, bar his legs. All the shots are now gone except one, and all wait, not daring to go near; then men, nippers, and a woman hurry down, the woman with a bottle and rags . . . and they raise the rock and lift him

on to the stretcher, fold his arms over his chest, and slowly six of them carry him past me'.

Streeton was at Lapstone and Glenbrook for nearly three months, and in that time two workers on the tunnel were killed and another seriously injured, 'at seven bob a day – the hardest work in the country for the money I'll bet'.

Of all Streeton's paintings, *Fire's On* is the one with the most intensity of light. It is as he describes it in a letter to McCubbin: 'the rock is a perfect blazing glory of white, orange, cream and blue streaks here and there where the blast has worked its force . . . I'll soon begin a big canvas (oilcolour) of this. I think it looks stunning. 'Tis like a painting in the "Burning Fiery Furnace"; so beautiful and bright and yet so difficult to attain'.

The painting was offered for 150 guineas in the Victorian Artist's Society Exhibition of May 1892, but it was not sold. In the next year it was bought in Sydney by the Art Gallery of New South Wales.

Facing Page:

The Selectors Hut;
Whelan on the log, 1890

oil on canvas
76.7 x 51.2 cm
Collection: Australian National Gallery, Canberra
Reproduced by permission of Oliver Streeton

Some of Streeton's most original and daring paintings came from his time in Sydney. The lover of the blue and gold countryside painted a view of the Old Redfern Station, then the terminus for Sydney trains, on a wet winter's day, where the only thing that shines is the slippery street. He painted it in three hours.

He experimented with long, thin paintings. *The Long Wave, Coogee* (9.2 x 54.5 cm) enables him to paint a whole great roller as it breaks; of course, in those days there was no surfer to take advantage of it. Coogee he described as 'a very jolly place, on warm days the place (which is like a nest) is filled with smiles and sweet humanity'. To Roberts he wrote: 'The ocean is a big wonder, Bulldog. What a great miracle. It's hard to comprehend it, like death and sleep. The slow, immense movement of this expanse moves one very strongly. You're made to clutch the rocks and be delighted, a dreadful heaving and soft eternity'. So in this long picture he combines the long wave, occupying almost the entire length of the painting, with the joyful figures on the beach at the far right end.

Facing Page:

Butterflies and Blossoms, 1890

oil on canvas
(on hardboard)
45.5 x 66.0 cm
Purchased with the assistance of a special
grant from the Government of Victoria, 1979
Collection: National Gallery of Victoria
Reproduced by permission of Oliver Streeton

In *Sirius Cove* he did something quite different, in a deep, thin vertical painting (68.8 x 16.8 cm) that has something of the qualities of a Chinese scroll painting.

Trying to find himself some fresh patronage, Streeton went to Adelaide in 1895. He deplored the boredom of Adelaide and sent a very amusing letter to S.W. Pring in Sydney: 'O! What a pious temperate uninteresting people they are'. He contrasts the 'orderly conduct of the populace . . . the old fashioned dress . . . the general prosperity and welfare . . . the carriages of the dull rich people . . . the temperate habits and early hours of these kindly conventional citizens' with lively, wicked Sydney. Finally he explodes 'Damme — there's —no sin here at all at all (sic)'. There were certainly no artists in Adelaide.

Eventually he found a rich squatter who took him to his grand house in Adelaide and showed him the paintings there which were all in water colour and clearly all imported. 'I never met such an artistic philistine — and yet he doesn't like pictures in oils. So I did no business'.

Facing Page:

Spring, 1890

oil on canvas
80.6 x 152.8 cm
Presented by Mrs. Margery Price, 1978
Collection: National Gallery of Victoria
Reproduced by permission of Oliver Streeton

In 1896 Streeton was back in Melbourne where he had his first one-man exhibition, at 88 Elizabeth Street, Melbourne. It was the custom in those days to charge an entry fee at galleries, and at one shilling a ticket Streeton made good money. And at last the National Gallery of Victoria bought its first Streeton.

It was a masterpiece, painted on the Upper Hawkesbury river, *Purple Noon's Transparent Might*. (The title was another quotation, this time from Shelley). There was a certain comedy to its acquisition. John Mather, a painter and Trustee of the Gallery, offered to buy it for the Gallery at the asking price of £150. The next day Langton, another Trustee, offered £126. Streeton wrote to Roberts: 'I told him (Langton) that I considered their 1st offer through Mather as being quite a serious one and refused, and a day or two later the said little "dingbat" left a note accepting it for £150. Ha! Ha!' It is interesting that it had been exhibited in Sydney two months before, for £210, but not sold.

It was painted from a rise known as 'The Terrace' between

Facing Page:

Gloucester Buckets, c. 1894

oil on canvas
28.0 x 51.6 cm
Gift of Howard Hinton 1933
Collection: New England Regional Art Museum, Armidale NSW
Reproduced by permission of Oliver Streeton

Richmond Bridge and Windsor. Streeton said he did it 'in two days and in a shade temperature of 108 degrees'. He later recalled working on it in a state of 'artistic intoxication with thoughts of Shelley in my mind'. The painting is pale and shimmering with a heat Shelley never knew, with the huge, cool river pool in the foreground.

In 1898 Streeton held another exhibition in Melbourne, which was very successful, and now at last he had the funds to travel. He had written to Roberts: 'I love Australia (and yet have seen so little) and shall be beastly sorry to go away (when I do go away) — Lord knows when or how. 'But I can't sit here thinking, 'tis waste of time.

In the same year of 1898 he did manage to 'go away'. He sailed to England and settled in the London suburb of Chelsea. In London he had a reunion with his old friend Charles Conder, whose dissolute life was reducing him to poor health. Streeton applied himself to painting and worked very hard. He sent a painting to the Royal Academy, but it was rejected. He could not sell his work.

At 34, when he should have been at the peak of success, he is

Facing Page:

Fire's On, Lapstone Tunnel, 1891

oil on canvas
182.9 x 121.9 cm
Collection: Art Gallery of New South Wales
Reproduced by permission of Oliver Streeton

writing to Roberts: 'my days have been rather dull and interspersed with miscellaneous blues. Fact is, last year I was lucky, and consequently did some of my best work; the past 11 months I've sold less than £40 (my exes. are rent £45, taxes about £20, caretaker, 5/- week, food, clothes, materials and cat's meat added on). Just managing to hang on, again and again'.

There was one tremendous consolation. He had met a girl, a Canadian violinist called Nora Clench. 'Ah! I get absolutely drowsy and faint with her sweet attraction when she is near . . . It's like finding another myself . . . She's much braver and finer in every way than I, and would have been a fit companion for Keats, I feel sure'.

However, in 1906 he returned alone to Melbourne. It was to a hero's welcome from his old friends. Professor Baldwin Spencer, the anthropologist, bought seven of his painting as soon as they were unpacked. He received an equally warm welcome on his return to Sydney.

In 1907 he had an enormously successful exhibition in

Facing Page:

Near Streeton's Camp at Sirius Cove, 1892

oil on canvas
30.4 x 22.7 cm
Bequest of Howard Hinton 1948
Collection: New England Regional Art Museum, Armidale NSW
Reproduced by permission of Oliver Streeton

Melbourne at the Guildhall, which yielded about £2000. He also sold well in Sydney. When everything was going so well for him in Australia, it was a tragedy for Australian art that he did not stay and ask his Canadian sweetheart to emigrate. But no, he returned to England, and married Nora in 1908. They spent their honeymoon in Venice.

Partly through the patronage of Nora's rich relations, Streeton was able to make a living in London for the next few years. During World War I he served in a medical unit and later as an official war artist. Although he had paid some short visits to his native land, he did not finally return to Australia to live until 1924, to settle on some land he had bought at Olinda near Melbourne.

There he painted heavier and cruder paintings which in the end were almost caricatures of themselves. In 1929 he became art critic for the Argus, and ironically was as reactionary a commentator on modern art as his predecessor Smith had been in the days of the 9 x 5 Exhibition.

Facing Page:

The railway station, Redfern, 1893

oil on canvas
41.0 x 61.0 cm
Gift of Lady Denison
Collection: Art Gallery of New South Wales
Reproduced by permission of Oliver Streeton

In 1924 he wrote to Roberts: 'We feel a little sad at cutting away, so to speak, from dear old Britain . . . She is the keystone of the world today. I think civilization depends upon her more than any other country'. But as with Roberts, Britain had sapped Streeton's artistic vitality.

He should have done what he had spoken to Roberts of doing, some thirty years before. 'If I can raise the coin I intend to go straight inland (away from all polite society) and stay there 2 or 3 years and create some things entirely new, and try and translate some of the great hidden poetry that I know is there, but have not seen or felt it'.

'It all seems to me like an immense bright sky enveloped in a wonderful mist waiting to be pierced here and there and have the glory of a "milky way" of modern intellect'.

But Streeton settled for respectability and polite society. He was knighted in 1937 and died at Olinda, Victoria in 1943.

Facing Page:

McMahons Point Ferry, 1890

oil on canvas
45.7 x 30.2 cm
Gift of Howard Hinton 1944
Collection: New England Regional Art Museum, Armidale NSW
Reproduced by permission of Oliver Streeton

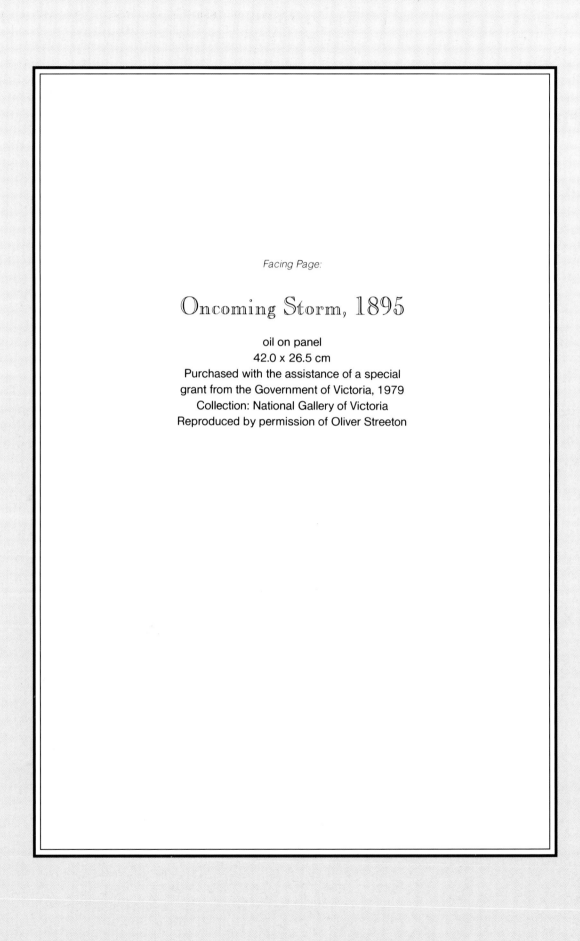

Facing Page:

Oncoming Storm, 1895

oil on panel
42.0 x 26.5 cm
Purchased with the assistance of a special
grant from the Government of Victoria, 1979
Collection: National Gallery of Victoria
Reproduced by permission of Oliver Streeton

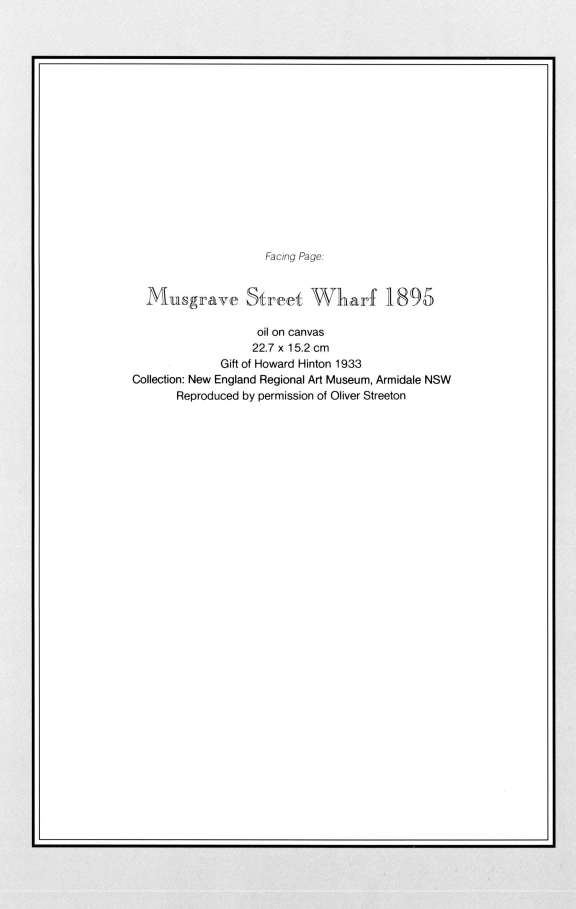

Facing Page:

Musgrave Street Wharf 1895

oil on canvas
22.7 x 15.2 cm
Gift of Howard Hinton 1933
Collection: New England Regional Art Museum, Armidale NSW
Reproduced by permission of Oliver Streeton

Facing Page:

Purple Noon's
Transparent Might, 1896

oil on canvas
121.9 x 121.9 cm
Purchased 1896
Collection: National Gallery of Victoria
Reproduced by permission of Oliver Streeton

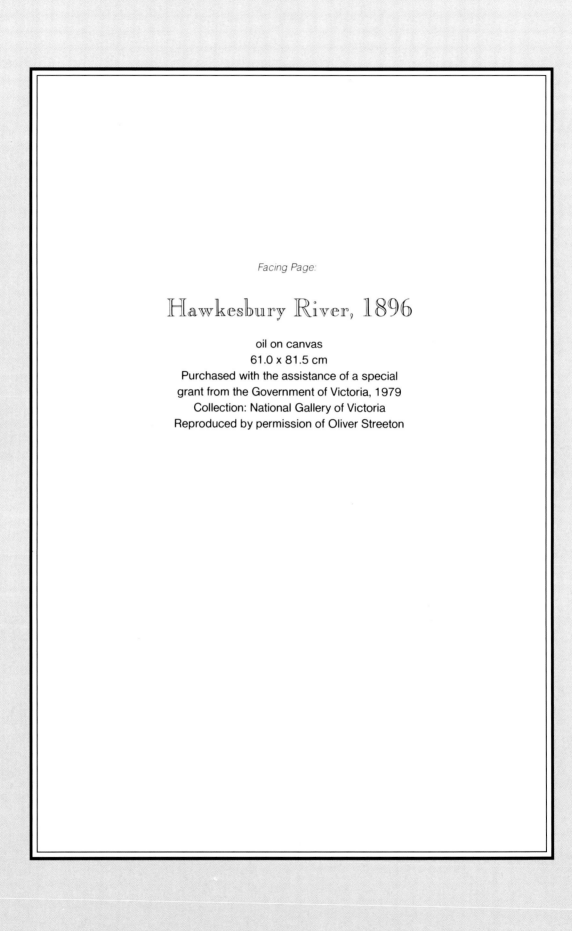

Facing Page:

Hawkesbury River, 1896

oil on canvas
61.0 x 81.5 cm
Purchased with the assistance of a special
grant from the Government of Victoria, 1979
Collection: National Gallery of Victoria
Reproduced by permission of Oliver Streeton

The Old Inn, Richmond, Hawkesbury River, 1898

oil on canvas
40.7 x 35.5 cm
Gift of Howard Hinton 1932
Collection: New England Regional Art Museum, Armidale NSW
Reproduced by permission of Olver Streeton

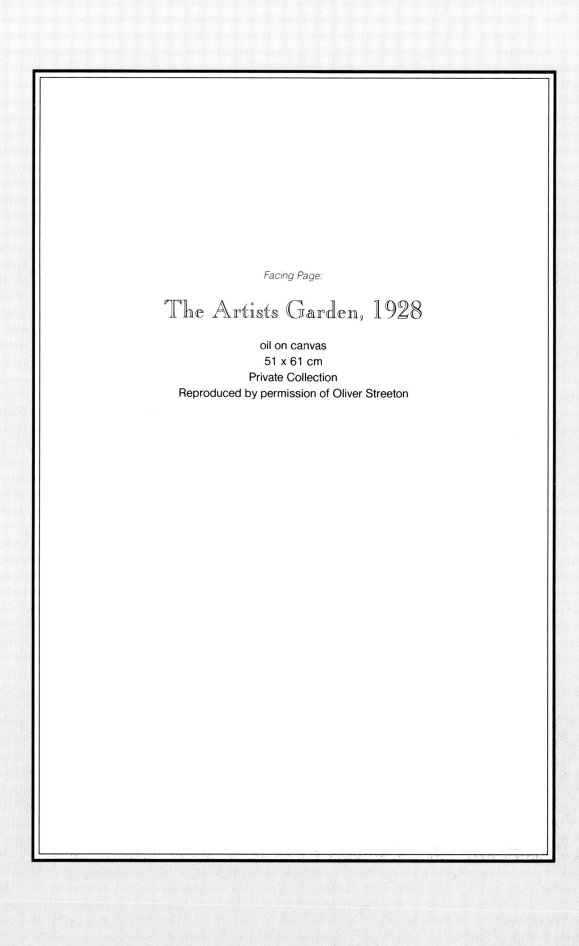

Facing Page:

The Artists Garden, 1928

oil on canvas
51 x 61 cm
Private Collection
Reproduced by permission of Oliver Streeton

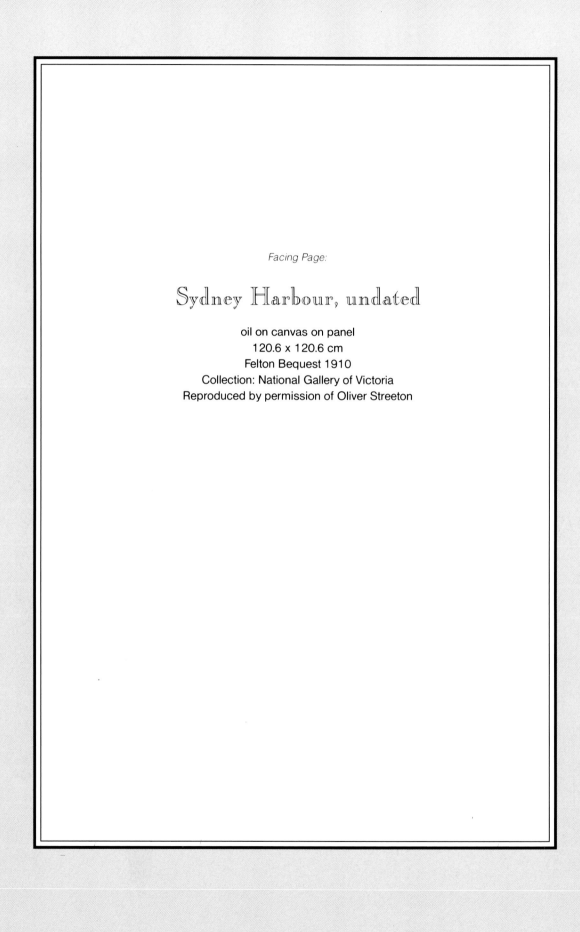

Facing Page:

Sydney Harbour, undated

oil on canvas on panel
120.6 x 120.6 cm
Felton Bequest 1910
Collection: National Gallery of Victoria
Reproduced by permission of Oliver Streeton

Paintings In Galleries

Early Summer — Gorse in Bloom, 1888
Art Gallery of South Australia

The Clearing, Gembrook, 1888
National Gallery of Victoria

The Yarra, Ivanhoe, 1888
Bendigo Art Gallery

Near Heidelberg, 1890
National Gallery of Victoria

The selector's hut; Whelan on the log, 1890
Australian National Gallery

Butterflies and Blossoms, 1890
National Gallery of Victoria

Spring, 1890
National Gallery of Victoria

McMahons Point Ferry, 1890
New England Regional Art Museum

Near Streeton's Camp at Sirius Cove, 1892
New England Regional Art Museum

Gloucester Buckets, c. 1894
New England Regional Art Museum

Oncoming Storm, 1895
National Gallery of Victoria

Musgrave Street Wharf, 1895
New England Regional Art Museum

Purple Noon's Transparent Might, 1896
National Gallery of Victoria

Hawkesbury River, 1896
National Gallery of Victoria

The Old Inn, Richmond
Hawkesbury River, 1898
New England Regional Art Museum

Land of the Golden Fleece, 1926
Australian National Gallery

Sydney Harbour, undated
National Gallery of Victoria